Canny Canon

2022 Expanded Abridged version

Copyright 1991-2022
October 26, 2022

George Wilson Freas II

First published by Supernal Publishing Services International

2022

Copyright © 2022 by George Wilson Freas II

Illustrations were created by the author using Midjourney (https://www.midjourney.com)

All rights reserved. No part of this publication may be reproduced, stored or transmitted in any form or by any means, electronic, mechanical, photocopying, recording, scanning, or otherwise without written permission from the publisher. It is illegal to copy this book, post it to a website, or distribute it by any other means without permission.

First edition

Table of Contents

Preface: 7
Canon: 11
Proverbs: 15
Prayers: 25
   Thankfulness: 25
   For Mealtime: 26
   For Others: 26
Poetical Rhymes: 29
Psalms: 33
Wisdom: 37
Philosophy: 41
Illuminating Questions: 45
About Heaven: 47
Puns to Enlighten: 49
Love and Making Sparks: 53

1- Canny Canon

Preface:

This book is a collection of realizations and inspirations that were accumulated during a period of over thirty years. One may ponder what truly is behind the human creative process and how insights like these are realized? How does inspiration occur? During the days of inspiration for this book, a typical day did not begin like: "Today will be a day to write some proverbs", or "The goal is to write a dozen witticisms today". During those days, 3" X 5" index cards were kept handy in the top shirt pocket with a black ink pen. When inspiration arrived, that day's date would be written in the upper right hand corner of the index card, and my own words were written in non-cursive English to dictate the initial version of the quote. Generally the quotes were revised after further thought in order to clarify the meaning or to make a wording revision. Never did the inspirations emerge in my mind directly as spoken words, but rather as a still small thought in my heart. This thought in some cases was multivalued, and did not equate to a single concept, but rather as a set of related concepts. It is like a tiny bubble that begins at the bottom of the sea, and as it rises to the surface of the sea it grows into a large set of bubbles. This tiny thought representing that realization or inspiration emerged through my mind and was written down in my own words on the index card. There are now several boxes of these index cards that remain, and they document this creative process. Through the years many different versions of this book emerged and were printed on my laser printer using my computer. At times, these new versions of the book were reproduced at local printers from my personal copy. These copies would be distributed to neighbors, or friends and family. Early on in the journey there was an effort to find a publisher for the book, so copies went out to various potential publishers. But the dissemination of the self-printed copies did not stop there. The manuscript was also distributed to famous personalities, TV talk shows and also the President of the United States as an act of good will and as a way to gain more external visibility. A publisher for the book was not found but the collection of quotes in the boxes of index cards still grew. Even today a box sitting is sitting in the computer room with several blank index cards, and a section with the newest writings, some of which made it into this expanded abridged version of the book. Being an abridged version, it represents a fraction of the total collection that appeared in one previous version of the book or another. So expect to see newer revisions or potential spin offs of this book in the future where some older quotes or writings and new material will be released. The illustrations in this book were created by the author using a software program called Midjourney. With Midjourney, images are created from a text description of the desired picture. Some of the illustrations were created using the exact words from the quotes in the book, adding a unique form of expression to augment these words.

Whomever reads this book, it does not matter what diverse walk of life or religious or non-religious ideology may be closely held, this book is for you. This book was assembled with the intent to enrich people's lives and potentially open hearts and minds through the words in the pages within it.

2- Canon

Canon:

A hypocrite says his brother is wrong when he does the same thing his brother does. A hypocrite says he is right when his mistake is just as great as his brother's mistake.

Man has vanity if he works with his hands; man has vanity if he does not work, but for the Lord. Man can only have vanity until his mind, body and spirit are one with the Lord. Then he is not a man, but an Angel.

It is not our importance or goodness that makes us worthy to go before the Lord, but our knowing we do not deserve to be worthy.

It would be better to be going against the wind and realize you are right, than to have wind at your back and awaken to the fact that you have always been wrong.

Do not try to be first and you will not be last. The ones that last are the ones that know to be first you must accept being last. It is better to strive to be what is best for the Lord and you will be first at His convenience.

The Lord is a Father of second chances, where the mistakes of the past may be forgiven.

The Lord needs us all to live up to our several abilities. If yours are being used for evil, then they will be severable abilities.

We cannot screen the part the Lord gives us in life, but we can play it out to the fullest.

If we were all equal, no one would be looked down upon, and there would be no one to look up to.

Only a wise man can retain integrity without sacrificing integrity.

You are not made righteous by another man's sin.

You must see the strengths in your shortcomings so they are no longer just shortcomings, but also hidden blessings.

There is a cavernous difference between someone who is crazy smart and one that is smart crazy.

No matter how old we are, it is not a crime to be young at heart.

Some truths are so ugly that the ones stating them are persecuted as being unjust for their statements.

Pray that all the ones you see laughing are laughing with you, not at you.

Please smile to spite the world's ugliness.

3- "Pray when you grow horns you are like a great horned owl!"

Proverbs:

You must just what is right, not right what is wrong.

It takes vision to not be blind.

We must all do good in deed.

Shed light, not blood.

Be a plant stake, not just another stick in the mud.

A branch starts out as a small bump on a log.

One that falls into a pit with snakes either becomes a snake, a mongoose, or dinner. We all should be mongooses in training.

Usually the one that looked too good to be true never was.

The Lord is the pilot, we are fortunate to be given co-pilot's wings.

If you do not talk to people, it will be almost impossible for them not to talk about you.

The disadvantaged have the best advantage, in hardship is much fortune.

We are strong when we tell the truth and say we are not strong.

Usually when someone cannot help themselves, that is what they do (help themselves).

Pray for good judgment so you will not fall prey to ones with bad judgment.

Do not push it, or it may come to shove you.

You cannot stare someone straight in the eye if you have two faces.

Someone else's dream dies when yours comes true.

Darkness needs light in order to make magic. Without light, there can be no magic at all.

People with straight laces do not skate.

Do not take just what is easy, or you will not be strong enough to take what is hard when you need to.

Even one that tries to make all the right decisions is a fool in some of them.

It doesn't matter if you lose, if you fight hard for what is right, then when you lose you still win.

Sometimes it is a part of our character to be out of character. What is out of character helps make our character complete.

If you are to be happy about someone being unhappy, please only be happy about them being unhappy for the right reason.

What you wanted is what you will not always get, but you will receive what you will need.

Some do not realize they are in trouble until they see how the trees are actually a part of the forest.

Before you can find your way out of the woods, you must see the forest as each tree you have bumped into.

Ones that become used to stepping on others become incapable of feeling for other's pain.

Some are overly interested in how pretty each letter of the law is.

To stop dancing madly backwards you must turn around, and fall flat on your face.

Idiocy is not justified by ignorance to its existence.

For some things, there is no way to be a 'Holy witness'.

If you are mad with someone, you only have one person to tell: the person you are mad with.

If someone needs to be mad at you, I hope you beat everyone to it.

After so long, the rose colored glasses will show faded roses.

The crystal clear glasses of a prophet are rose colored to all else.

A flea on a dog's back is good to the flea, but hell for the dog.

The early bird eats worms, while the rest take whatever they get.

Some that go overboard will be put there literally.

It would be better to have a clouded mind that knows the truth, than a clear one that only believes lies.

When we are young, our parents tell us where we cannot go, and when we are old, our children do.

One that is ordinary, is loved more than one that hurts others to be a cut above the rest.

You cannot light the fire of one you do not hold a candle to.

You cannot ask anyone else to live by your own words if you cannot live by them yourself.

If it were not for mistakes, there would be no incentive to do better.

A diamond cannot refine itself if it perceives its own sparkle already to be perfect.

Beware that the delight for the good in you does not make you evil.

Prepare for the worst and expect what words cannot describe after a long hard struggle.

The door that swings both ways is the one that is used the most. The straight gate only swings one way.

Those that stay on another's back can only be a lion, not a lamb.

You cannot cry like a lamb if you are a wolf on another's back.

You have to be half baked before you can hear: "well done".

With Religion, we all must have that certain way about us.

The pit that evil is bound in is the void it creates in people's lives.

Some build a moat around them, and say it is the mote in other's eyes.

The moat people have to cross is the one in their brother's eye.

Ones pleased because of the twinkle in their eye, may be persecuted as though it were a mote.

If you rebuke someone for the beam in their eye, your eyes may not be beaming.

Pray when you grow horns you are like a great horned owl!

If you give 110% of yourself, you lose nothing when you tithe.

The Lord cannot dwell in a temple that is worshiped more than He.

There is a difference between cheating, and doing what is allowed.

When it comes to the wicked, we all need to have little words (few and non-praise worthy).

One who has issued an ultimatum has placed one on their own shoulders.

Faith is what keeps us from what we do not do, and what makes us do what we cannot keep ourselves from doing.

No sin is justified, but some mistakes may be unavoidably just.

Do not take just what is easy, or you will not be strong enough to take what is hard when you need to.

If you would not die to do what is right, you will live a life without just meaning.

Do not try to retain dignity, when it is given away for humility, it is replaced with His security.

It is better to tell the truth about your feelings than to have soothing words as to deceive.

It is better to show that you are mad at your friend, than to lie to them and make them your enemy.

It is better to have a poor spirit that knows how to fight, than a full, complacent spirit that expects everything given to them.

It would be better to fight with only a part of you, than to give up and always have nothing.

One that fears their destiny may wrongfully cling to paradise's path, fulfilling the destiny they fear.

Improper reaction to fears can cause fears to be real.

The evil one took the cake, so now it is not a cake walk for anyone.

Sometimes it takes a broken neck to get your head back on straight.

When you get things off your chest, the Lord gets things off your back.

Often the only thing wrong is that you have too many things right.

The heat is hotter if your feet have never been close to the fire.

You can be taken to nowhere by trying to keep someone else from getting somewhere.

Do not worry if someone else is better than you, your reaction could make them always better than you.

Beware of climbing to a high pinnacle, it may be the tack you sit on.

An evil mind that is sharp is like a wasp's stinger.

There is no way to feel guilty, if you never see that you have done wrong.

There is a difference between what delights evil, and the wrath of the Lord.

You have to agree to going on the hard road before you get to the easy one.

So many of the have nots are the ones that have it all.

You must give it all away before you can have it all.

Those that have nothing, are the ones that end up with it all.

If you admit the way you are nobody, you become somebody.

Pray to receive of the abundance in the world that the Lord wills you to receive.

Do not be too alright to be alright.

Man's conceit is bred by his own devices.

A part of me could not want to make me or another part of me eternally lost.

Just as pure love fuels righteous lives, the wicked need perversion.

It would be better to be hungry than to have too much to eat, and no place to go when you die.

What evil wants is for all of us to be afraid or repulsed by what is best for us.

Leave no stone unturned, it could be the first stone cast at you when it is turned.

Do not try to cover mistakes, but try to see the good in them and make them blessings.

We will hit the mark in the end, but miss it until we get there.

No one here can fill the shoes the Lord has for us until the hereafter.

We must have shoes our children cannot fill in some ways, but prepare them to fill a pair made especially for them.

To many, the most vain conversation is of the most worth.

Some things are worth crying about, and some things are worthy of hate.

The Lord giveth, and evil taketh away (all it can get).

The Lord did promise evil a woes garden.

A good apple that was bruised falling off the apple cart is preferred over one that will always be sour.

What you may do to keep from facing a small mistake could be the worst mistake you ever make.

4- Prayers

Prayers:

We have to tell the Lord where we displease Him, so He will not tell us.

Thankfulness:

For this day, I say: Amen, to thank You, Lord for the light You send. I have the honor to stand in Your light, and upon this, I can depend.

I thank the Lord I awoke today, that I may see Your Light and You can hear me pray.

I thank You for my adequacies, that they are sufficient to overcome my inadequacies, with Your help.

Lord, I am thankful that You have shown me where there is dark in the light, and the light in the dark.

Lord, thank You for the gifts You have bestowed upon me in this world. I pray my life may be a gift to You and to those of this world.

Lord, guide us, direct us, heal us and protect us. I pray for those that love me, those that hate me, and all those in between. May all of us do Your perfect will, knowingly and unknowingly.

For Mealtime:

For this meal, I say: Amen, to thank You, Lord for the bread You send. I have the honor to break Your bread, and upon this, I can depend.

We are grateful that the Lord has granted us these gifts of grace.

We thank You for the bread of life that sustains the breath of life.

Lord, may this food help enable me to go where You will me to go.

Thank You Father, for the hands that prepared this meal, and for those here, that we all may know of Your perfect love, that we may become the people of Your kingdom according to Your will.

We break bread for life from the bread of life. Precious bread sustains precious life, thank you Lord for this life.

By His grace we may eat this food, by His grace He does provide, we thank You Lord, we are alive!

For Others:

Lord, I pray that Your abounding Love will grow in all people.

Lord, make wise the rich to help feed the poor.

May the voids in my life be filled by the voids in other's lives through fellowship and service to You.

Pray for someone to step forward and answer the prayer of one that is praying.

5- Poetical Rhymes

Poetical Rhymes:

Yesterday, today was tomorrow. Tomorrow, today will be yesterday. Watch it, or your todays will become yesterdays, and you will know not what to expect tomorrow.

It has been the vogue to be a rogue, now the fashion should be compassion, the words of a sage must be the rage, please love and care to gain savoir faire, and go the extra mile to be in style.

It would be better to be with an obedient ox than to be with a conceited fox.

The brotherhood of brother hoods does not want your brother good; they will sway him from the sainthood, and tell you it's for the common good.

I hope you see those real lies with your rational eyes so you will realize why people rationalize.

If you do not tell irrational lies, you will not have to rationalize.

Before our officials declare immunity to obtain impunity, it should be irrefutable that the charge is imputable.

If you hesitate, you may be exacerbated that you procrastinated.

Please look before you leap. I would rather be belated and elated than berated and hated.

The Lord does love it when we do not covet.

You need to be forward with the froward.

Senseful eyes spy lies as unwise.

We need to practice humility to the best of our ability.

It is an abomination to be a botheration.

It is the Lord's advice to give up every vice.

The Lord is the one that validates if you truly have valid hates.

The ones that will not recompense will be put behind a fence. The ones that will not reconcile will be overcome by a crocodile.

The ones that belittle may always be little.

The ones that give a lie for a lie and a truth for a truth may give an eye for their lie and a tooth for their half-truth.

The Lord will awe men that say amen.

6- "as a myriad of crystal winged butterflies"

Psalms:

Oh Lord, I am but an insignificant part of Your great creation.
But yet, at times, You turn Your love and gaze upon just me.
You guide and reprove me to conform to Your ways.
In the eternity of what is to be, the only way I can repay Thee,
Is to magnify the reflection of You ingrained in me.

Because of all I am not, I am awed at what I am.
What I am not, is the totality of everything else.
The totality of everything else is the entirety of the Universe,
But what I am is a small human on earth,
Loved by the divine maker of the entire Universe.

Lord, make straight my ways,
Be the sextant on my journey of life,
Protect my beloved from the grasp of the wicked,
Shine Your light upon our path,
Guide us from all evil harm,
Think not that You may forsake us,
But lead us in Your Holy ways.

Thanks, Oh Lord for Your love that heals,
Grace and kindness for broken hearts,
Wholeness is treasure beyond perception,
A gift received only from You,
Please take our hearts to Your safe house (Heaven).

Your perfect ways protect Your beloved.
Though their agony feeds wicked desires,
Perseverance makes Your beloved strong.
Brokenness makes Your people mend.
Your loving spark is all they need,

For them to defend Your truth and righteous ways.

Lord, our torments are your comforts,
Our comforts are your worries,
Our anguish is a humble beginning,
Our delights could be a haughty end,
A world of hurt where life exists,
An eternity freed of pain and sorrow,
Sheltered lives, not prepared for the hereafter,
Abundant hardship evokes Your pity,
With sickness, the hope of conversion,
With prideful decadence, surety of damnation,
A prophet's sackcloth chimes bells in Heaven,
Finest clothes glint of Babylon's luxury,
And sincere intentions offered to You,
Feel just to demand Earth's comfort,
Please, Lord rebuke what is evil,
And show each the good rugged path.

We are so insignificant,
But oh so majestic.
Less than a speck in a vast expanse,
But each moment our body has countless movements.
We must tremble when we ponder the Lord,
With awesome splendor knowing we came from Him.
An inconceivable privilege is the capacity to know,
And just as inconceivable is how much we do not know.
We do not understand the privilege of understanding,
Without understanding we would not know love.
What is it to know?
How does man perceive?
When man perceives and understands
Why he has the gift of perception,
He will know why there is a Heaven,
And why he was made like the Lord.

Blessed is not powerful or overpowering, but as fragile as a bird's egg.
Blessed is not profound but is obvious as a silent falling feather.
Blessed is not intense, but like the gentle mist at the bottom of a waterfall.
Blessed is not strong, but as a soft light upon a fragile antique globe.
Blessed is not dazzling, but as a myriad of crystal winged butterflies gently fluttering in rays of light.
Blessed is not stimulating, but like a peaceful flag lapping in a placid breeze.
Blessed is not covetous, as it flows freely from the creator's universal love.

7- Wisdom

Wisdom:

When it rains, the things you saved for a rainy day bring you thunder.

It is never better to be late for forever.

There is no future in living like there is no tomorrow.

Roll with the punches, throw few of your own.

There is more hope for one that is spoiled rotten, than for a rotten spoiler.

When a need arises, your complacent wants must go away.

Do not try to be the best in any category except the one that contains only yourself (everyone needs to refine themselves).

The ones that put up insults will be judged for their injury.

If everything is going right, you must be doing something wrong.

If you know you need something and do not want it, you may not survive.

Ones that seek vain glory will be vain and inglorious.

Those without righteous conviction may be righteously convicted.

Some people think that money buys happiness - all anyone needs is love and a just purpose in life. If you disagree, you may need to adjust your purpose.

Some people are beside themselves because they believe they are the only one's worthy enough to walk next to themselves.

The only handicap you need is your thinking cap kept nearby.

Anyone that hinges their success upon someone else's failure is that, a failure.

Sometimes it is wiser to put someone into the deep freeze before they become rotten to the core.

Some people say they would lie to change the way things are. But if you lie, you will be in chains and it will change into a scar.

Watch for the ones that look for loopholes that can become nooses.

The easy road is usually the primrose path, and is always a dead end.

If you are a sore loser, you may have been born one.

The ones that cannot pay their dues will have the blues.

In the business world, many climb the totem pole with telephone service man's boots on.

Some people, instead of putting their foot down, put it in their mouth.

Generally it is hard to persevere when the damage to your purse is severe.

It will be too late for the ones that continue to say it is.

Ones that continuously put their noses into other people's business would be better off putting it into a rat trap.

When someone finds their bugs, they sometimes must choose between the lesser of two weevils.

Some well laid plans make mice of men.

If you look for greener grass, you may end up on the rocks with sage grass until you are a sage.

It does you no good to be Johnny on the spot if you are on the wrong spot.

You may be sick if you realize that what you are becoming is not becoming.

8- Philosophy

Philosophy:

Sadness: The state of observing a part of you being less than what it needs to be, or it being lost, and the human reaction to this observation.

Happiness: The state of observing a part of you being what it needs to be for yourself or others, and the human reaction to this observation.

Joy: The state of observing a part of you being what others could not be, for their sake or humanity's sake, and the human reaction to this observation.

A 'part of you' may be defined as:
1) What you believe in.
2) What you do.
3) What ones close to you do.
4) Ones you love.

With relative truth you know nothing.

There are degrees of not knowing, but only one absolute truth.
1) You suspect something is true
(gut feel, little evidence).
2) You believe something is true
(an amount of circumstantial evidence).
3) You truly believe something is true
(it has not been proven to you yet, but facts infer this to be true).
4) You know something is true
(your experiences are facts, and are irrefutable).

Reality is the current state of flux of meaning with respect to absolute truth.

(Good / Bad) Luck is synchronicity that (minimizes / maximizes) entropy in some way.

All general rules are invalid in some way, except this one.

Everyone is foolish or seems foolish from some view of reality.

Everyone is mad (or insane) from some other person's view of reality.

Bad:
Religion for self-satisfaction or with the goal of making yourself better than others.

About love and money:
  Render unto Caesar mammon (money).
  Render unto the Lord manna (love).
  The richer will be richer, the poorer will be poorer, we choose the categories in which we will be wealthy.

Hopefully you are to be wherever you are. It is harder 'to be' if you are not there when you are there.

The existence of candle light to a cave dweller is more profound than the International Space Station flying over in the nighttime sky in the eyes of a modern man.

May all the black spots in your life be like commas or the periods in sentences: they blend in, and cause a pause before going on.

Too much practice can make even a perfectionist too weary to do a perfect job.

The most favorable path for the overall good is usually the most difficult to navigate.

9- Illuminating Questions

Illuminating Questions:

Are you to dance for your soul, or because you have one?

Is your rut caused by too many pillows, or too many hard places?

How many times in life are we like a rookie in little league: asleep or daydreaming without the ball, and too self-conscious with it?

When a tinker fails at making a new creation work, does he blame the creation for its error?

How many hope chests become so weathered and worn, the owners are afraid to look into them anymore?

Just as the rainbow has all spectrums of color in it, each of us are a single ray in that bow, and the Lord is perfect white. What would the rainbow be like if a dark spot is in it?

Do you consider preening the fruit until the right picker comes along? Or have you picked fruit because evil would take advantage of it, if you did not?

Are you happier when the spider catches a roach and not a butterfly?

Are not the weeds happy when and if they can grow more rapidly than the good in the grain?

If a weevil gets into the flour and makes a nest and prospers, is the weevil just? It thinks it is. Is the owner of the flour unjust?

Are you a puppet, puppeteer, or one of the audience? If you are in the audience, do you see through what the puppeteer is doing, or are you a puppet in that way?

10- About Heaven

About Heaven:

Love is the manna fest in Heaven.

The only type of liar that is allowed into Heaven is one spelled: lyre.

Heaven is like a fine box containing sugared candies and pastries. Nothing but sugar plums will dance therein.

Heaven is a clean room that is free from disorder and sin where everyone loves and trusts one another.

Love is Holy and should be blessed by the Lord.

We all would be happier if Angels only had to save ones that passed out from sheer delight.

11- Puns to Enlighten

Puns to Enlighten:

The tour on the Judgment day will be to the Museum of Ancient Hiss stories, or the Museum of Modern Hearts.

The Prince of Larkness will defeat the Prince of Darkness.

A person that thirsts for righteousness is like a hound dog after a fox.
  It is the Lord that says: 'I Saint nothing but a hound dog. '
  The evil will attempt to: 'taint nothing but a hound dog. '

An open mind sometimes indicates a lost marble.

An open mind allows one to rearrange or augment their marbles.

We must strive our entire life to be wholed.

The ones that have lost their salt can only be sincere about their insincerity.

I would tell some people to swallow their pride, but nobody is strong enough to give them the Heimlich maneuver.

You must try to make the title of your life not be: Gullible's Travels.

One day you may be Humptey Dumptey and take a great fall, and if you are rotten enough, no one will bother to pick up the pieces.

The camel's back was broken by the needle it had to go through to get into Heaven.

Sometimes we need a gnat in our lives to strain the humpfs from a camel.

There is treasure in solemn men's minds.

Do not set your sights too high in society, you may find yourself up the clique that furnishes no paddles.

The evil sows care-away seeds.

12- Love and Making Sparks

Love and Making Sparks:

Each intimate relationship is a liability, it is both person's responsibility to make it an eternal asset.

Commitment papers-Marriage Certificate

When cupid's arrow strikes, it does not hit the heart, it goes right through your head.

Make sugar, without raising cane.

You must be slow like a turtle before it is right to be like a rabbit.

Before super glue can form a permanent bond, both surfaces must be clean.

We are held responsible for the twinkles in our eyes.

We all need just hugs.

The home should be a safe container for 'cherish able' goods.

When you met someone new, have you ever thought: 'I could be crushed if you do not have one'.

A couple's life together should be half to be wholed.

Put only good into the quiver of your beau.

You and your spouse should have a quakey (make the earth move).

It is easiest to light a sparkler with one that is already lit.

You have to stick out your neck in order to neck.

When you let it all hang out, make sure you do not get it dirty.

Your spouse should be your rest queue.

There are more ways than one for your hummingbird to take off.

Some people hold a grudge (in the arms of one disliked by their enemy).

Sometimes it takes the arms of a new love around you to remove the knives from your back.

The Rules:
Staying between first and second bases is safe.
Stealing third base to keep evil from stealing home base is still illegal.
A home run is out of the ball park.
The short stop should be where to stop short.

First and second are usually the bases almost missed, and third and home are worn out.

Please remember that in each moment we are making memories, and that it is more important to have memories we are not ashamed of, than to have the very best ones. Many people are like they are sleep walking. Are you ashamed of what you do when you are sleep walking?

The eternity of a moment:
A moment is an instant, immeasurable as eternity and as timeless as all time. There are moments that last an eternity, and eternity's that are wholly contained in a single moment. It is best not to live

together, but to always live when and where you are together.

We have a responsibility to one another and to the Lord to give a place for our talents and our loved one's talents to grow. The power of love can heal anything.

Your walk in life with your mate is like a three-legged race. You both must work together like a perfectly tuned machine. Being intimate with another is like letting them put their leg into your rope. You cannot walk together like that.

Try being a cupcake: these cakes can be eaten without cutting them.

www.ingramcontent.com/pod-product-compliance
Lightning Source LLC
Chambersburg PA
CBHW070858050426
42453CB00012B/2257